AF472171

ENCOURAGE YOUR SOUL:
It's Not As Bad As It Seems

VEL HUMBERT

WESTBOW PRESS
A DIVISION OF THOMAS NELSON & ZONDERVAN

WestBow Press books may be ordered through booksellers or by contacting:

WestBow Press
A Division of Thomas Nelson & Zondervan
1663 Liberty Drive
Bloomington, IN 47403
www.westbowpress.com
1 (866) 928-1240

ISBN: 978-1-4908-4058-1 (sc)
ISBN: 978-1-4908-4057-4 (e)

Library of Congress Control Number: 2014910561

Printed in the United States of America.

WestBow Press rev. date: 6/25/2014

This book is dedicated to everyone, regardless of your religion, that you may come to know Jesus Christ for yourself and establish a never-ending relationship with Him.

If you are not a believer, hopefully you will become a believer and ask, “What must I do to be saved?” Perhaps you have strayed away from God. Read this book and you’ll learn that God never takes a break from you. The Bible says, “He will not leave you nor forsake you” (Deuteronomy 31:8 NKJV). Maybe you just need to be encouraged. Your faith will see you through if you just believe. Believing in Jesus Christ is essential in order to benefit from the experiences written in this book.

I say to all, take the parts you need and share them with others, that they may be encouraged and know they are not alone. The Word of God has helped me in the past and is still helping me today. I thank God for the opportunity to share these experiences with you. May the grace of our Lord and Savior, Jesus Christ, guard your hearts and minds, and keep you in perfect peace. Amen!

Contents

Introduction

This book was inspired by God. Fictional characters have been used to demonstrate real-life situations that you may have experienced, are encountering now, or may face in the future. As you read the stories, ask yourself, *Can this be me?*

The purpose of this book is to encourage and give hope to anyone that has experienced or is going through a rough time. It was not the experiences that brought each character through that determined the outcomes, but how each character handled the situations. Knowing and applying the Word of God were instrumental in overcoming the issues in each story.

All things are possible through Jesus Christ (Matthew 19:26; Mark 10:27). There is a positive in every negative, and you can't convince me otherwise. You just have to find the positive. Is the glass half full or half empty? You choose. Although it may appear that some of the chapters overlap, each chapter is designed to bring a different perspective.

Can These Dry Bones Live?

You might be wondering, "Dry bones? This doesn't make sense. What are dry bones?" They are situations that keep holding you back. They are trials and tribulations that weigh you down so much, you think you can't go on. Sometimes you are ready to throw in the towel and give up. Sounds familiar? I've felt that way many times: choosing a husband, dropping out of college early after barely getting started, getting divorced, being scared to live alone, for fear of not having enough money to pay the bills. Am I hitting home yet?

How about relationships with men? Maybe you thought a man would help you, but instead you wound up getting hurt or abused and had to deal with a lot of unnecessary drama. What about letting people live with you, like family members and friends? It starts out for one month and then turns into a year or more. Then they have the nerve to say they're doing *you* a favor, or say, "If you want me out, you need to get an eviction notice"—even when they're not paying any rent!

Let's take a look at Joyce. This strong, confident, independent black woman who could hold her own was going through the "go-throughs" of life and trying to hold on. She first had to recognize that these experiences were keeping her down and killing her slowly. These were her dry bones.

In the Bible, God asked a question: "Son of man, can these bones live?" The response was "O Lord God, You know" (Ezekiel 37:3 NKJV). These next lines are important. God says in verses four and five, "Prophesy to these bones and say to them, O dry bones, hear the word of the Lord! Thus says the Lord God to these bones. Surely I will cause breath to enter into you and you shall live." Do you get it? To prophesy means to speak; after all, God spoke and things happened. If you don't believe me, check the record for yourself by reading Genesis 1:3, 6, 9, 11, 14, 20, 24, 26. Each verse starts with "Let there be," "Let the," or "Let us" (NKJV). You get it yet? Don't worry. I'll tell you. God spoke and then it happened, and in the same way you can speak life into your dead situations, your dry bones. Or you can be like the walking dead with no direction or purpose, only existing.

Joyce made excuses for her situations. No one had forced her into anything. She had convinced herself that she needed to do what she did because it was right for that moment—never mind the consequences. Everything she did came out of her ability to choose.

The choices we make are ours, and we have the ability to choose right or wrong. As Deuteronomy 30:19 says, "I have set before you life and death, blessing and cursing; therefore choose life" (NKJV).

Joyce found that she had been acting out of her emotions. As she got older and more mature, she became wiser and began making better choices and decisions. She began to realize that excuses may explain, but they do not excuse. Let me give you an example; let me make this plain. Your baby needs diapers, and you go to the store to get them but don't have the money to pay for them, so you leave the store without paying for them. You get caught, the police are called, and you are arrested. You are asked, "Why did you steal those diapers?" Your response may be "Because my baby needs them, and I have no money." Well, you just explained the reason, but it does not excuse you from breaking the law. So you see, excuses explain but do not excuse. The choice is yours.

Joyce was twenty-seven years old when she made a conscious decision to go back to church. She'll never forget it. Her children were giving her more problems than she could take, and she had become overwhelmed and needed relief. She started out saying, "I'm going back to church as soon as I get myself together." Little did she know; that was a trick. She never really got herself together, because it was always one thing after another. First she needed some decent clothes and shoes to go to church, so she purchased them. Next her children needed decent clothes and shoes for church, but she didn't have the money. But once she got the money, something else was always more important. Sound familiar? The harder Joyce tried to meet the needs of her family, the longer it took to initiate her plan to go back to church. It was always something.

Then, out of the blue, she said, "We're going just as we are." This thing called "life" was really getting her down, and she had to do something about it. So off to church they went.

By that time, Joyce had a made-up mind—she was going to get as much as she could from the Lord, and her desire grew more and more. That's probably what kept her sane. She came to realize you have to feed your spirit the same way you feed your physical body—garbage in, garbage out. What you take in the most is what you become. Her way of doing things was not working, so she had to find a new way, and she chose the Lord.

Joyce and her children joined a church and started participating in the different ministries within it. Did everything in her life become easy after joining church? No. But it sure did make a difference in how she handled things. You know, the Bible says, "Wisdom is the principal thing; therefore get wisdom: and with all thy getting, get an understanding" (Proverbs 4:7 NKJV). Joyce started reading and understanding the Word of

God and learned how to apply it to her everyday life. Did she always get it right? No. But she knew that the God she serves is long-suffering and forgiving. Thank God for another opportunity to get it right!

Joyce was baptized before she was eight, sang in the choir, and helped teach Sunday school and Vacation Bible School. You might remember those days. As she got older, her reasons for going to church changed. First, it was because her mother made her go. Then she was going to see her friends and boys. And she got money: her mother would give her fifty cents to put in the offering basket, but she would spend twenty-five cents on candy and put the other twenty-five cents in the basket. The point is, Joyce's mother trained up her child in the way she should go, so that when Joyce grew old, she would not depart from it (Proverbs 22:6 NKJV). But when Joyce turned eighteen, she left the church. You know how it was. She was grown and wanted to do her own thing. She didn't really have the Lord on her mind, but she's certainly glad He had her on His mind.

If you could only see Joyce now. She is a grown woman with children and two grandchildren she adores. She can appreciate all that her mother instilled in her, which led her right back to where she started, rooted in the Lord. I hope by now you got it. All of Joyce's understanding of the dry bones came from the foundation laid when she was a child. It never left her. She was able to pull it out and use it to regroup. As an adult, she is able to reflect on her childhood and remember the importance of spiritual growth and development. She is able to return to what was instilled in her the most. She also knew she couldn't raise her children by herself. She needed help, as nothing else worked.

Living without Christ is like being a child without a parent. At the time you accept Christ, you are a new creature and a babe in Christ. According to 2 Corinthians 5:17, "Therefore if any man be in Christ, he is a new creature: old things are passed away; behold all things are become new" (KJV). You have to nurture your spirit just like you nurture your physical body. Your physical being gets hungry, so you feed it. Well, your spirit gets hungry too, and it needs spiritual nourishment. This is accomplished through the Word of God. To properly develop and learn to apply the Word of God to your everyday life, you need to be trained through studying and praying for wisdom and understanding. "Study to shew thyself approved unto God, a workman that needeth not to be ashamed, rightly dividing the word of truth" (2 Timothy 2:15 KJV).

Now that you have been enlightened, read and answer the following questions. Be honest with yourself. After all, this is to help you get through the go-throughs of life.

Questions to Think About

1. Where are you right now in your relationship with God?

2. Have you called on the Lord and how did He help you get through the situation that was holding you down?

3. What did you gain from the experiences you read about?

4. What will you do differently to help you through?

Why Do I Keep Doing the Same Thing?

Ever wonder why you keep going through the same thing over and over again; Things never changing, always staying the same? Sure, you want better for yourself, but you keep going around in circles. Sound familiar? Then you ask yourself, "What am I doing? That ain't right! How did I get here?" Then, all of a sudden, it hits you. You get a revelation, and back down memory lane you go. How many times does it take before you get it? Let's see!

Let me introduce you to Joan. She was twenty years old and married. She had her first child at the age of twenty-one. Ten months and three weeks later, she had another child. She married a man without a job. Ladies, a *big* mistake; she was doomed from the start. Of course she didn't listen, being happy at that point, she told her father, and he was not supportive. This man had nothing; I mean nothing to offer except, well, you know. Joan didn't want to hear anything anyone had to say. She was all alone in her own little world.

She lived in a basement, literally—concrete floors, old brick walls, spider webs, dirt and dust—yet she made the best of it; however, she was too embarrassed to invite anyone over. She didn't want her family to see how she was living. The bathroom and tub was "cruddy," not just nasty. She wouldn't dare take a bath or even sit on the toilet. But she still made the best of it.

There were times when they didn't have food. They lived with his family, and it was every man for himself. She can remember having $3.18 back then, enough for a TV dinner for each child. As she fed them, she drank a little of the gravy to curb her own hunger pains.

At that time, her husband was no help. He talked a good game, but that's all he did. He stayed out all night running his illegal pharmaceutical business and was terrible at it. He never had any money to take care of his family. And she was too embarrassed to let her family know what she was going through. (You know how some families are. They are always waiting to say, "I told you so.") Joan would even visit a close family friend and spend the whole day there, just so the children could eat. She knew she would at least feed them, and she didn't have to ask, because she was too embarrassed.

For a while, she wondered why she stayed in the marriage. She had a job, but she had trusted him to keep the money that was supposed to be for getting them a place to live. And he spent all the money (and it was her fault for giving it to him). Again, ladies, a *big mistake*; trusting someone who never had nothing! Don't get me wrong; there was some happiness. They used to party together, and as long as both of them were together, it was okay. But let her say she was hanging out with her girlfriends, and it was all over. They would argue sooo much that she'd changed her mind and not go. Am I down your street?

He said the same stuff you hear on television: Baby, I'm sorry. I love you. You know I never meant to hurt you. And the old favorite: I'll never do it again. It seems like that should have been the time she left. Nope! She stayed. You know why? "Because I love him." She fell for the okeydoke.

By this time, Joan didn't have a real relationship with God, so she didn't realize that she could call on Him. Yes, she knew Him, but she had very limited "word power." You see, Joan did not read her bible and did not know much about scriptures. She may have known the basics but she didn't know the power and meaning of scriptures. And she certainly did not know how to apply it to her situation. Now that Joan has grown spiritually, she is able to look back and she finds herself singing that often-sung line from *Sanford and Son,* "What kind of fool am I?"

Some men always have a story for why they need money. And how about a man in jail? Yeah, Joan was once seeing one of them. It's not like she had a boyfriend at the time. What harm could it do? After all, people in jail are people too, and they need someone to talk to. Now, let me be clear: Joan knew him before he was incarcerated; he had been her boyfriend in the past. He just happened to call (collect), and she broke her rule and accepted the charges. What did she have to lose?

Boy, he talked a good game, and she had convinced herself that all the good men were either dead or in jail. They would talk and laugh, and she could share anything with him. She even talked to him about boyfriends. And when she wanted a man's opinion, she asked him. Time went by—years went by—and they grew closer. She started sending him a small amount of money; he didn't have to ask for it. Then she sent more and more money; no pressure from him. Then it happened. She was convinced that he had a chance to be released. They had numerous conversations about paying for a lawyer for an appeal she knew he couldn't win. By this time, she knew the Lord. She had returned to God and her relationship with Him was growing. However, she didn't seek God about any of her relationships.

Here's another one: she bought a car to help her man get to and from work. She didn't give it to him; she just let him use it. She wasn't that dumb! She fell for that line, and this time he preyed on her being a Christian and going to church. What did he do? You guessed it: he started going to church too. Then he changed up. But you can't keep faking the funk; the real you will show up eventually. What about always wanting to support him, but he never wants to support himself—or you for that matter? And he can always find fault in you. What about that?

This time Joan sought the Lord and asked Him to show her that man's character in a short amount of time. It usually took her a year to find him out; this time it took four months. She listened to God and got him out of her life quickly. Of course he didn't like the outcome, and he threw three plants through her front window. But he suffered the consequences, and it wasn't pretty. Six months later, some family members and friends caught up with him and they gave him the biggest beat down. She didn't approve of the method, but he got the message. A little over a year down the road, he apologized to one of her family members. Had she been obedient to God from the start and not let him live with her, she would not have gotten the plants thrown through her window and the additional drama of others becoming involved.

These experiences are presented to help you see that sometimes people make dumb mistakes and bad decisions. If it weren't for that, Joan would not have felt the need to call on God. She knew to call on Him because she was brought up in the faith. One day, the Holy Spirit was speaking to her as she was going up stairs. She said, "Okay, Lord, I give up!" At that moment she realized she could no longer do things her way. The prophet Isaiah spoke for God, saying, "For my thoughts are not your thoughts, neither are your ways my ways, saith the Lord" (Isaiah 55:8 KJV). Joan began to realize that she and God do not think the same way or act in the same manner. And she was willing to throw in the towel.

Kenny Rogers sang, "You gotta know when to hold them, know when to fold them, know when to walk away, know when to run." Joan had had enough, so she gave herself up to God. She knew she couldn't win. Now, how long did it take her to see that? About twenty years. She had to surrender; she didn't have a fighting chance against God. And He is such a gentleman that He stepped out of the way and let her do it her way. She had to surrender, and the moment she did, God began to work in her, on her, and through her.

We all have to do the same thing. We must surrender all to God, both our will and our ways.

If you haven't yet, I dare you to try Him. God has a plan for your life. He said, "Before I formed thee in the belly I knew thee; and before thou camest forth out of the womb I sanctified thee" (Jeremiah 1:5 KJV). God, who knew you before you were even thought about or born, care enough about you to save you from yourself. I encourage you—no, I urge you—to try Him. Let God reign over your life, and you will see that He makes the difference. Also read and reread the Scriptures that are referred to in this book.

I'm not saying you won't have problems, because we all do. I'm saying God will make the difference. He will give you inner peace to help you get through. That's why you can call on Him in your weakest moment.

Don't be so tuned into your problems that you shut God out. Be a living witness for God. He will give you peace way down in your soul. This will make the bad stuff not so bad and the good stuff better.

Questions to Think About

1. Where are you right now in your relationship with God?

2. Have you called on the Lord and how did He help you get through the situation that was holding you down?

3. What did you gain from the experiences you read about?

4. What will you do differently to help you through?

What Do I Do When I've Tried Everything?

Veola was experiencing problems with her second marriage, which was only a year old. Things were happening that she hadn't anticipated. As the wife, she was trying to merge two families into one. Little did she know she would be in it alone. She didn't tell anyone about how she felt, including her husband.

In the beginning, she chalked it up as everyone needing an adjustment period. She was rationalizing in order to get over the day-to-day hurdles. The children needed to adjust, the parents needed to adjust, as a married coupled they needed to adjust, and even relatives and the children's friends needed to adjust. So Veola just went along to get along. She tried hard to overlook the foolishness, and in spite of it, some days were good.

But just as she thought it was getting better, things got worse. She brought some of her concerns to her husband's attention, and he acted as if nothing was wrong—or maybe he didn't see anything wrong. To him everything was going right, just as he wanted, she supposed. On top of that, her feelings did not count to him at all.

Further down the road, she concluded he didn't care. She even second-guessed herself, saying, "Maybe I'm making a mountain out of a molehill. Maybe it's me and not them." Their day-to-day lives continued, and they looked like the perfect couple to those on the outside looking in. They had no clue, or so she thought. Then she would get little comments like "I told so-and-so that he had to respect you." And "you know, he loves his children"—as if she didn't love her children. And "if I had a wife, my children would know she is in charge; they would have to respect her."

Veola also discovered she had more structure in her life than he had; he was in free fall. His children had no responsibilities or accountability; they didn't help out around the house, and they didn't care. When her own children saw this, they didn't want to help out either, and quite frankly, she wasn't going to ask her children to do anything he wasn't willing to ask his children to do; it would not have been fair. Yet she knew everyone should do his or her fair share to help out.

All these children were grown—accept one. And the youngest did whatever she wanted to do without repercussions. Veola's son became so disrespectful to her that she had to ask him to leave—to move out. Her children knew she was not going to take foolishness from them, yet they saw her taking foolishness from the other children. They even asked why she allowed it. She explained to them as best she could: when you are in a marriage, you have to take into account the other children, and you just can't abruptly change everything at one time. They took that explanation for a minute, but it wasn't good enough.

Everything was fine when it came to her paying the bills, she was a good wife. When it was time for the banquets, going to church, shopping, getting him out of debt and building his credit, getting the car he wanted in her name, and giving him money—oh, she was definitely a good wife. Don't forget the anniversaries; she made sure they went out of state every year for three years straight. The fourth year they didn't go anywhere; they couldn't, because money had become too tight.

By now, they had been married for four years, and you would think by then everyone would have adjusted. Well, things had gotten worse. Veola had worn a mask for four years, and she just couldn't do it anymore. And he wore a mask like never before. She learned that he was a master at "faking the funk." He would go along just to get what he wanted from her, his family, and friends, though he would never admit it. One might say he was a manipulator.

Veola didn't see this in the beginning. She thought he was an "innocent victim," which is what he portrayed himself to be. Looking back over the marriage, she could see that she was happy one out of the four years—not one entire year, but pieces out of each year to make up one year. She always said to him, "I'm second to everything."

For example, sometimes they would be spending time together, watching TV, and he would get a call from a family member. He would answer the phone right where they were resting and say, "No, I'm not doing nothing." Veola would think, *What am I, chopped liver?* After he got off the phone, she would tell him how she felt—"You say you're doing nothing?" He would say, "Aw, babe, it's all right." Then he'd get up, saying, "I'll be back." He'd go make his runs with this, that, and the other. That was his answer for everything: "Aw, babe, it's all right."

One might ask, "Well, did she talk about the things that bothered her?" The answer is yes, but to no avail. You see, Veola's husband did not like confrontation. He did not want to discuss anything when asked. She asked if he wanted to go to counseling, and he answered with a definitive no. She told him she felt all alone in their marriage, and she got *nothing!*

The final straw for Veola was her feelings of wanting to do harm to her husband and children. She wanted to get even and pay them back for making her feel like she didn't belong and she didn't exist. She knew she had to do something to keep her sanity. One Sunday afternoon, between church services, she *really* knew what she needed to do; she just *had to* do it. So she said to him, "I think it's best we separate." He replied, "If that's what you want." That's it! Nothing more!

All Veola could say to herself was *Wow, that's all I get?* That was the worst thing: she felt like she had gotten nothing from him—no fight to keep the marriage—absolutely *nothing!*

Veola had a hard time with the decision to separate, but she felt it had to be done in order for her to have peace of mind and to stop feeling all alone even when surrounded by the entire family. There were periods of loneliness and feelings of distance. She had no peace within, and it wasn't getting any better. She had been placed on the back burner during the entire marriage, disrespected by his children and their friends, and even had to battle with her own child, who she had ultimately asked to leave.

A month later, her husband and his children moved out. She was determined to make it a smooth transition, but he kept nitpicking. She finally called her girlfriend and made preparations to stay at her house while they moved. Her oldest son stayed at the house to make sure everything went smoothly for them. She returned when all of them were gone. She was so relieved when she came home to an empty house. She didn't care; she needed peace of mind. Her son brought his bed out of the basement for her to sleep on, and he slept on the sofa in the basement. Her other son gave her his old television set. And she was okay.

She was now alone with her thoughts and God. At first she didn't know what she was going to do with herself. She had mixed feelings; she was glad, yet sad, hurt, mad, angry, and a little confused. Sometimes she didn't know how to feel. But all in all, she was relieved.

In Veola's relief, she was still mad that her husband had not thought it was important to fight for the marriage. This made her think, *Why did he even ask me to marry him, and why did God confirm it to me.* She began to rationalize the reasons behind what she was going through. The more she thought about it, the madder she got, and the more she wanted to get even with those "jerks," as she commonly referred to him and his children.

Veola had her good days and her bad days, but she still had to function through it all. It wasn't easy. She had to go to work with these feelings and deal with and support other people who had problems themselves. Some of her coworkers were licensed counselors, and she confided in them. They weren't just any counselors; they were Christians. And this was important to her, because she too was a Christian.

One counselor just listened and allowed her to talk, giving no input at all. At first Veola wondered about that, but now she understands that listening was all she needed at that time. Another counselor asked her if she wanted to save her marriage, and she thought for a moment and said yes. But all her efforts had not helped at all. She had to realize his motives for marrying her were different from her reasons for marrying him. She married because she loved him and wanted to spend the rest of her life with him despite their differences, and they both loved the Lord. They were in it together, or so she thought.

He had married her to get everything he didn't get from his previous marriages. Veola made him feel real good about himself; repaired his credit, which changed his status; and was a showpiece when they went out, especially when he performed marriage ceremonies and had to preach. He took all that she could give him: her heart, her love, her finances, and her peace of mind. She discovered she was fighting a losing battle and was, quite frankly, too tired to try again.

Veola was also mad at God. I mean *terribly* mad at God, and she never acknowledged it openly; she often said it in her mind, but never out loud. You see, she loved the Lord and knew His voice. Jesus said, "for they know his voice. And a stranger will they not follow" (John 10:4–5 KJV). She knew she clearly heard from Him. Hurt and upset, she would ask Him, "Why did you allow me to marry a man that really did not want to be married?"

Then she began to second-guess that she had heard from God. She went back and forth with herself about that—back and forth and back and forth she went for months. On and off, she asked God, "Did I really hear from You?" Then she was reminded again of a Scripture: "for they know his voice. And a stranger they will not follow." That still didn't keep her from being angry with God.

Why was she so angry? Because God knows all and sees all; He knows what will happen before it happens. She couldn't believe that God would lead her to such a state that she felt like she had lost herself.

One day at work, Veola was talking to a coworker, a fellow Christian, and out of her mouth came "I'm mad at God!" Then, amazingly, she heard a voice say, "That's all I've been waiting to hear." The Holy Spirit began to speak to her and referred her to a Scripture. She read it and began to get understanding: "and with all thy getting get an understanding" (Proverbs 4:7 KJV).

My point is, she had kept things to herself, even when it came to God. Nothing happened until she admitted out loud that she had a problem and that the problem was with God. She never disrespected God, but she had an unresolved issue she could not get past; she couldn't move on. Once she released it, God was able to give her revelation about her situation, and she felt so much better. All of a sudden, she wasn't mad at God any longer.

Veola had been holding on to that anger for months, being eaten up inside with no relief. She had to admit her anger openly before getting resolution and being released. She was bound by her situation, and it was making her bitter. I'm so glad she was listening in the Spirit, for now she is free. "He who the son sets free is free indeed" (John 8:36 KJV). "He that hath an ear let him hear what the Spirit saith to the churches" (Revelation 2:7, 11, 17, 29; 3:6, 13, 22 KJV).

Questions to Think About

1. Where are you right now in your relationship with God?

2. Have you called on the Lord and how did He help you get through the situation that was holding you down?

3. What did you gain from the experiences you read about?

4. What will you do differently to help you through?

How Do I Handle the Unexpected?

A forty-seven-year-old African American married woman went for a routine checkup before having a minor procedure done at a local hospital. She received a phone call from her doctor, who said, "Vivian, your urine pregnancy test showed positive." But she had not even known a pregnancy test was done! She laughed. Her tubes had been tied and burnt for twenty-five years, and her primary care doctor confirmed that a tubal ligation procedure was irreversible. She said to the doctor, "This cannot be!"

The doctor ordered additional blood work and said he would notify her on Tuesday. It was Friday. What a long weekend she had! Her feelings ranged from happy to sad, but were mostly mixed. She cried a little. She wanted to tell her husband, but was reluctant.

She finally got herself together and began thinking, *What a blessing; children are a gift from God. This is a miracle. What God has given us, He will make provisions for.* She began to smile, and she decided to tell her husband.

Vivian started by saying, "I got something to tell you!" You know every time you start a sentence with "I got something to tell you," it usually means something is wrong. So her husband asked, "What's wrong? Are you pregnant?" She began to cry and explained what the doctor had told her. Her husband held her and comforted her, saying, "It's going to be all right."

She was excited as she anticipated the unexpected and she was sad, not wanting to hear, "it was false positive." Told you—mixed feelings. Sometimes she didn't know what to feel or how to feel. The more she thought about it, the more she was able to embrace what she hadn't wanted in the beginning.

By then, it was Monday. How would Vivian get through until Tuesday? It helped that her husband supported her and the outcome, one way or the other. Knowing that God was in control also helped her through. If she was pregnant or not, it was predestined, because God knew His plan for her life. She couldn't help but wait in anticipation, hoping and praying for a positive result on the blood test.

Because God was in the equation, she was able to see things in a new light. She was not concerned about this or that. She knew God would make a way somehow. Now for the results: the blood test was negative. How did she feel? You guessed it: mixed up all over again. A part of her wanted a baby with her husband; however, there was a sense of relief. Whew!

As she looks back, Vivian knows it was for her good that they didn't have a child together. Trying to make the best out of the situation would have caused a bigger problem in the end.

Time had passed, and Vivian had been married for four years. What an experience! She was so busy trying to give everybody the benefit of the doubt that she was suffering. She tried to unite their blended family, and that's why no one knew the house was just in her name. It had to be; his credit was "messed up." She wanted to get him to where she was financially, so they could do things together.

It was she that carried the health insurance so he could have a normal paycheck (only receiving half). It was she that paid off his back taxes (these taxes were before they were married). Don't misunderstand; she wanted to do these things and more, but she was being drained physically and emotionally. He even accused her of not being supportive of him and his children.

Things were not working out from where she stood, yet she encouraged him to get his high school diploma, and she sat at the computer doing his online classes—while he sat beside her dosing off. She paid off his debts, helped his son get a vehicle repaired for inspection, and took in his daughter when she abruptly came to live with them—though it was never discussed with her. The house had more people than rooms to sleep in. But again, she was accused of not being supportive. I bet she was important when it came to money!

She was even used when it came to saying no to his family, because he couldn't. You see, *no* was not a part of his vocabulary. She's the one that didn't get any support from him: no understanding, no empathy, and no response to her concerns. He even had the nerve to say he wanted things to be like they were when it was just him and his kids. Never mind Vivian and her children—"they didn't matter" (his words). What a nerve! Vivian finally had enough, and he had to go. Even then, he had nothing to say; he didn't even flinch. Now Vivian was devastated; her marriage had come to an end.

Now a decision had to be made, and it was very hard. Since Vivian knew she was not reconciling with her husband, and there was no chance that he would even make an attempt, the next thing was a divorce. But to her, divorce meant the end—that's it, nothing more! She had to deal with it before it dealt with her, knowing divorce would have an effect on her emotions, if she let it.

Why should she hold onto someone that didn't want her? He wanted marriage on paper, the perks of having a wife sitting in the congregation, going to banquets, handling finances, giving him money, buying suits—the whole works and all the perks.

When she told him she would be filing for a divorce, his response was "Okay." Well, another opportunity to try and work things out; but she got nothing! So Vivian moved forward and she called this the stages of divorce:

First, you have to admit that the marriage is over with no chance of reconciliation. Only you know when it's over. This is important when you believe in the sanctity of marriage. You don't get married to end up divorced. You take your vows very seriously.

Second, you have to decide you want a separation and then actually separate. It's one thing to say you want something; it's another thing to act on what you said. The act means something is really happening to your marriage; without a doubt, it is over. In Vivian's mind, this had to be in order for her to move forward and begin the healing process.

Third, you have to confront being by yourself, alone. Vivian knew it was coming, but was she prepared? Not really. You see, she and her children had been together for twenty years, yet she thought she was by herself. As they became young adults, they were doing their own thing, staying out, and sometimes not coming home at all. Yet she had come to realize that really wasn't being alone. Now that she was alone, she didn't like it. But she handled it because she had no choice; she refused to go through again what she had just come out of.

Vivian had told herself and God that this was best in order to keep her sanity. Near the end of her marriage, she had become bitter, angry, hurt, upset, disgusted, and disappointed. She wanted to pay people back for the pain she was feeling. She spent a lot of time talking to God and encouraging herself. Often her feelings of hurt showed on her face, and God used other people—the pastor and his wife, coworkers, and her best friend—to help and console her.

It had been four months since the separation. She lent her car to a friend and was dropped off at work. Right in her job's parking lot, it hit: a nervous breakdown. It was the worst experience she ever had. She was out of her comfort zone; she had lost all control. For the first time, Vivian didn't know how to escape. She was trapped within herself, with no place to go, nowhere to run or hide. She cried continuously and didn't know why. She couldn't stop.

It happened without warning, and it went on all day and into the night (from about eight in the morning until ten at night). It was the longest fourteen hours she had ever experienced. Where did it come from? Well, as she reminisced, she began to see her entire life from age eighteen to the present. She looked at the relationships she'd had, and she saw that everybody expected her to be strong. Ask Vivian to help; she'll do it; she can handle it; bring her the drama, and let her fix it; she'll figure it out. Little did she know that everything had compounded and had finally come to a head.

She didn't tell anyone except her best friend. He was with her through the entire ordeal. She prayed and cried, cried and prayed. It was like a never-ending moment for her.

How did Vivian get through it? It was such an awful feeling; it felt like depression. She was in her darkest place, and she didn't want this thing called life anymore.

No, she didn't want to commit suicide; she just wanted to escape the pain and agony of what she had been through. She was ready to give up everything: her home, her car, her family. She wanted to scream, "Just leave me alone!" Her experiences through the years had caught up with her, and she was done. She just wanted to go away, leaving everything behind.

Vivian finally called on Jesus. Her prayer was short, for she was too weak to do or say anything else. But she still knew enough to call on Him. You see, it was after she called His name that she got relief. As Jesus said, "I am the way, the truth and the life" (John 14:6 KJV). That's why it's very important—a necessity—to know God's Word and have it in your heart. *No word, no power!*

Vivian was able to call on the one she knew she could depend on, Jesus. Yes, her best friend was there, and he was trying to keep her out of the hospital and give her a sense of hope. He did more for her that day than anyone—except Jesus. You see, he had his own issues and rightfully he should have left her, but he didn't. God used him to help her, and she was so grateful.

By late evening, Vivian had calmed. She recited a Scripture while lying in bed, and she fell to sleep. When she woke up the next morning, it was as if nothing had happened. She was rejuvenated, refreshed. You would not have believed it unless you'd seen it for yourself.

Vivian had slept peacefully. "The peace of God which surpasses all understanding shall guard your hearts and minds through Christ Jesus" (Philippians 4:7 NKJV).

She knew when she woke up that she was okay. Now you see why the Word is important. I urge you to get in the Word, and you too will feel the presence of God in your everyday life.

After being separated a little more than a year, Vivian filed for a divorce and paid for it. That brought on another kind of feeling: a little hurt, but mostly relief. You see, she wanted nothing from him and she knew it was over.

Sometimes she reflected on her marriage, trying to figure out what had happened, what went wrong. However, she continued to encourage herself, talking to God constantly. She had questions, and God gave her answers. She had dealt with her feelings before the divorce became final, or she would have been doomed to repeat the pattern of feelings all over again when she received the divorce decree.

In the midst of everything she was going through came the unthinkable; Vivian's son was brought up on charges she could never imagine. He had just come home in 2010, after being incarcerated for two and half years, and she was glad to have him home. He came home with a plan to do the right things. He took care of his business with very little guidance. He mapped out everything he wanted to do, and he did it. She was so proud that he finally had a sense of direction. He bought a car, got a job, and obtained his commercial driver's license in a matter of a few months.

But then he was arrested and incarcerated with no bail. After a little over a year, he went to court. People tried to prepare Vivian, but she had no idea what to expect. She didn't understand the magnitude of the charges. It was unreal, yet as real as it could get. It was the straw that tried to break the camel's back. It was the icing on the cake, and it was thick and heavy.

Finally, the trial was over, and he was sentenced to more than life. Vivian couldn't believe it. He was still in his twenties, and she felt like she had suffered a death. Yet she tried to keep it together. She had her moments, good and bad. She would go back and forth about the sentence, but when she compared what she heard on the news with her son's sentence, she saw the injustice. Not only was she dealing with that issue, but her other son was treating her like dirt. If you knew Vivian, you wouldn't believe it. It was as if he had no home training, and that was bothering her too. Everything was hammering her simultaneously.

Those two years took their toll on Vivian, and she experienced mini breakdowns. She had had it! As much as she had tried to deal with the issues of life, life had been dealing with her. She didn't want to accept the fact that depression was trying to overtake her, and she kept fighting. Then one day, she had another breakdown—the "big one." The pain she was feeling made her want to give up everything: no more work, home, or people. She wanted to be left alone, to leave the state, and to start over where nobody knew her. She wanted no help from anyone. "Just leave me alone." But what was she really going to do? Life was still kicking her in the butt, and she just couldn't take it anymore.

Going to church became harder, but she went. She found herself waking up in the middle of the night, talking to God, praying for her children, praying for herself, and asking for peace of mind.

Every time she watched television, something reminded her of her children—especially the one with the more-than-life sentence. Every time someone was convicted of a crime and sentenced, she would compare the outcome with her son's. Then she would analyze it, and before you knew it, she was consumed with his situation. She would ask herself, *How can it be? This person killed somebody and was sentenced twenty-three years, but my child, who did not kill anyone, received more than double life.* Then she would hear another person's sentence and conclude the same. This went on for months, and without even thinking about it, she was thinking about it—if you know what I mean.

She had thoughts about how other children were treating their parents. She compared the lifestyles of her children and the lifestyles of some of their friends. She gave her children love and support, nurtured them, and gave guidance, directions, hugs, kisses, encouragement, discipline—everything they needed and some of what they wanted. Vivian couldn't understand why her child would treat her with such disrespect. She did the very best she knew how to do, and for some reason, that was not enough.

Then she did what everybody says not to do: she questioned herself as a parent. She had not done anything wrong when raising her children, so she wondered why they had gone off the deep end. She went back and forth in her mind, wondering what had happened. She became consumed, and though it was overpowering her, she still couldn't help wondering what went wrong.

Vivian kept going to church. It was a struggle, but she went. She had good moments, bad moments, and those moments in between her moments—most of which was consuming her. She cried out to God, and some days she didn't know what to say. Aren't you glad He knows our every thought?

One day during pastoral anniversary week, her church had revival services, and she attended Wednesday through Friday. (She missed Tuesday.) On Wednesday, the pastor preached a sermon called "You Just Don't Know." After the service, she thanked the pastor and told him it was for her. "You just don't know, *literally*!" she reiterated.

A real whopper happened on the last day of the revival, Friday. The preacher preached about thorns in the flesh and spoke from 2 Corinthians 12:9 which reads as follows: "And He said to me, My grace is sufficient for you, for My strength is made perfect in weakness" (NKJV). Vivian immediately could relate to the preached word and began to say to herself, *Okay, you've been looking at this thing all wrong! Your problem situations—you've looked at them all wrong!* She understood that in God she had strength, and she could get through the go-throughs of life. Her eyes had been on the wrong thing, and she was sinking fast. That preached word reminded her of who she was in the Lord, for in Him, "I can do all things through Christ who strengthens me" (Philippians 4:13 NKJV).

The Word of God is supposed to bring life to a dead situation, yet Vivian was falling fast. She had taken her eyes off God and hadn't realized it; she had been consumed with the issues of life. Remember what happened to Peter when he walked toward Jesus on water? "So He said 'come,' and when Peter had come down out of the boat, he walked on the water to go to Jesus. But when he saw that the wind was boisterous, he was afraid and began to sink" (Matthew 14:29–30 NKJV). He took his eyes off Jesus just as Vivian had, and she was too sinking. He certainly kept her from drowning.

She was transformed instantly that night. Now she is free in her spirit, and she can truly say she has been transformed by the renewing of her mind. God said to her, "Keep your *focus*. I'm here. Get rest, enjoy life, have fun, but most of all, stay focused on Me. I got you and your children. I'm up all night anyway. Let it go. I'm here!"

She was instantly reminded that "if the Son makes you free, you shall be free indeed" (John 8:36 NKJV). God told her, "No more therapy; you are delivered." And she thanked God for using the others to bring forth a word that set her free. Now she says, "I can truly say I'm happy in Jesus alone."

Questions to Think About

1. Where are you right now in your relationship with God?

2. Have you called on the Lord and how did He help you get through the situation that was holding you down?

3. What did you gain from the experiences you read about?

4. What will you do differently to help you through?

5 How Do I Encourage Myself?

To be encouraged is to be lifted up, to get an extra boost, a push that can move you to a better place. Webster's Online defines *encourage* as to inspire with courage, spirit, or hope; to attempt to persuade; urge.

When you know who you are and whose you are, you can make it. How do I know this? I read my Bible. It is the foundation for my life, and you must believe it is the foundation for your life too. According to Genesis 1:27, 28, 31 God created man in his own image, in the image of God created he him; male and female created he them. And God blessed them. And God saw everything that he made, and, behold, it was very good (KJV). I know who I am in God. I am fearfully and wonderfully made (Psalm 139:14 NKJV). I am a descendant of the Lord, Jesus Christ (Romans 4:18 NKJV). I am an heir and joint heir with Jesus Christ (Romans 8:17 NKJV). You gotta know who you are, believe who you are, and know God knows best (Jeremiah 1:5 NKJV).

I have presented various life experiences. Through them all, Jesus was the answer. But what do you think happens when your mind is on your problems? You see, just because you are a Christian does not mean the humanity in you is gone. After all, we are all human; we all get caught up in our sorrows.

There is a common factor in all these experiences, and that is Jesus. Do you know that life issues can cause you to lose your mind—literally? But Jesus is really the way, the truth, and the life (John 14:6 NKJV). We can all identify with the Joyces, the Joans, the Veolas, and the Vivians. I, myself, spent a lot of time talking to God and encouraging myself daily with positive thoughts and words, often saying them to myself, speaking life to my own dead situations. I often wore my feelings of hurt all over my face. And you know what they say about hurt people: they hurt people. That's where I was for a while.

I'm keeping it real. Much like Vivian, I wanted to hurt the ones that hurt me. All of them were going to get it; I didn't know how yet, but I was working on it. But thank God for Jesus and a relationship. You see, if you really have a true relationship with Jesus and you've made Him your lifestyle, you are always tuned into Him, whether you want to be or not. I could hear that voice (the Holy Spirit) saying, "Vengeance is Mine, I will repay, says the Lord" (Romans 12:19 NKJV). "I'll make your enemies your footstool. Thou preparest a place before me in the presence of mine enemies" (Psalm 23:5 KJV). You know what? That's all I needed to hear, a word from the Lord. If I wasn't listening and then being obedient, they would have won. I would have lost everything. Instead, I gained everything: my peace of mind, my joy, and most important, myself.

By the time I received my own divorce papers, I had dealt with the reality of things, and now that I'm legally divorced, I'm really okay. In my mind, heart, and soul, I'm fine, wonderful, and fantabulous! I'm ready to move on.

I was ecstatic and anxious to move along this process. I first had to change my name back to Humbert (my maiden name), wait for the new card to come, and then go to Motor Vehicle Administration with my Social Security card and the original divorce decree. I then realized I also needed to change my name on my bills and at work. Man, I was on a roll, feeling some kind of good. I started with the creditors, faxing copies of my driver's license along with a written request to change my name.

After doing all that, I remembered, *Girl, you gotta change all your user names, not just the one at work!* So I got busy. I pulled out the sheet with all my user names and passwords, and one by one, I changed all that I was allowed to change. I wanted no reminders of that life. Then I said, "You gotta inform your coworkers." That meant even people at our sister sites, vendors, and friends. Boy, I was doing it, and it felt grrrrreat (like Tony the Tiger)!

I sent an e-mail to everybody, giving them the ability to call me directly if they had questions or concerns. People were calling me and sending congratulations. It was hilarious! Most of the ones that responded knew what I had gone through. I got a big smiley face and plenty of laughter. Talk about encouragement!

I got the ball rolling, and it kept rolling. I was cracking up all by myself. I even changed the name tag on the wall outside my office door. I typed my name in my computer and tried to get as close to the font size and style as I could. Then I cut it out ever so neatly and taped it over the old name. My door stayed partly open, and as people came by, they could see my new name. At times, I even modeled my name, positioning my hand as if I were presenting it (the way they do on *The Price Is Right*). And I was, *me*!

One of my coworkers that had provided me support and helped me through the storms asked how I felt. My response was "I am fantastic, fabulous!" I had already dealt with this final stage, and I was better than great; I was fantabulous.

Oh, one more thing: I had to change my name on my voicemail, as I was politely reminded. "You have reached the voicemail of Vel Humbert, formerly Vel Flight ..."

I was tickled to death. All day long I laughed with people and especially by myself. I really loved me, and it felt real good. You might be saying, "What in the world? How could she be laughing? Well, it wasn't easy when I was going through it, but since I've gotten through, I've earned the right to laugh; I'm entitled, and I deserve it.

Make no mistake; I could not have done it without God. The joy came from God; the strength came from God. Remember, for the joy of the Lord is your strength (Nehemiah 8:10 NKJV). I can do all things through Christ who strengthens me (Philippians 4:13)! Yes, I'm smiling right now!

Each experience reminds you that with God "all things are possible to him that believes" (Mark 9:23 KJV). The key to encouraging yourself is your focus. Any time you intervene, doing things your way, you lose the battle and your focus. But the good news is that it's not over until God says so. That means you have another opportunity to get it right. How do you do this? By listening to God, the Holy Spirit, and following His directions. His Word says, "I will never leave you nor forsake you" (Hebrews 13:5 NKJV). Jesus Christ is the same yesterday, today, and forever (Hebrews 13:8 NKJV). That's the wonderful thing about Jesus. As much as we don't listen and then choose to do our own thing, He still gives us another opportunity to get it right.

Remember, God is a gentleman. He will step aside, allowing you to do it your way. And when you've had enough and call on Him, confessing that you are tired of doing it your way, He will intervene and get you back on track. When you are ready to throw in the towel, it's good to know He is waiting with open arms to receive you and me and take over.

Questions to Think About

1. Where are you right now in your relationship with God?

2. Have you called on the Lord and how did He help you get through the situation that was holding you down?

3. What did you gain from the experiences you read about?

4. What will you do differently to help you through?

www.ingramcontent.com/pod-product-compliance
Ingram Content Group UK Ltd.
Pitfield, Milton Keynes, MK11 3LW, UK
UKHW040020200726
13854UKWH00001B/277

9 781490 840581